Editor-in-Chief and Founder:
  Lyndon H. LaRouche, Jr.
Editorial Board: *Lyndon H. LaRouche, Jr. , Helga Zepp-LaRouche, Robert Ingraham, Tony Papert, Gerald Rose, Dennis Small, Jeffrey Steinberg, William Wertz*
Co-Editors: *Robert Ingraham, Tony Papert*
Managing Editor: *Nancy Spannaus*
Technology: *Marsha Freeman*
Books: *Katherine Notley*
Ebooks: *Richard Burden*
Graphics: *Alan Yue*
Photos: *Stuart Lewis*
Circulation Manager: *Stanley Ezrol*

INTELLIGENCE DIRECTORS
Counterintelligence: *Jeffrey Steinberg, Michele Steinberg*
Economics: *John Hoefle, Marcia Merry Baker, Paul Gallagher*
History: *Anton Chaitkin*
Ibero-America: *Dennis Small*
Russia and Eastern Europe: *Rachel Douglas*
United States: *Debra Freeman*

INTERNATIONAL BUREAUS
Bogotá: *Miriam Redondo*
Berlin: *Rainer Apel*
Copenhagen: *Tom Gillesberg*
Houston: *Harley Schlanger*
Lima: *Sara Madueño*
Melbourne: *Robert Barwick*
Mexico City: *Gerardo Castilleja Chávez*
New Delhi: *Ramtanu Maitra*
Paris: *Christine Bierre*
Stockholm: *Ulf Sandmark*
United Nations, N.Y.C.: *Leni Rubinstein*
Washington, D.C.: *William Jones*
Wiesbaden: *Göran Haglund*

ON THE WEB
e-mail: eirns@larouchepub.com
www.larouchepub.com
www.executiveintelligencereview.com
www.larouchepub.com/eiw
Webmaster: *John Sigerson*
Assistant Webmaster: *George Hollis*
Editor, Arabic-language edition: *Hussein Askary*

EIR (ISSN 0273-6314) *is published weekly (50 issues), by EIR News Service, Inc., P.O. Box 17390, Washington, D.C. 20041-0390. (703) 777-9451 ext. 415*

European Headquarters: E.I.R. GmbH, Postfach Bahnstrasse 9a, D-65205, Wiesbaden, Germany
Tel: 49-611-73650
Homepage: http://www.eirna.com
e-mail: eirna@eirna.com
Director: Georg Neudecker

Montreal, Canada: 514-461-1557

Denmark: EIR - Danmark, Sankt Knuds Vej 11, basement left, DK-1903 Frederiksberg, Denmark. Tel.: +45 35 43 60 40, Fax: +45 35 43 87 57. e-mail: eirdk@hotmail.com.

Mexico City: EIR, Sor Juana Inés de la Cruz 242-2 Col. Agricultura C.P. 11360 Delegación M. Hidalgo, México D.F. Tel. (5525) 5318-2301 eirmexico@gmail.com

Canada Post Publication Sales Agreement #40683579

Postmaster: Send all address changes to *EIR*, P.O. Box 17390, Washington, D.C. 20041-0390.

Signed articles in *EIR* represent the views of the authors, and not necessarily those of the Editorial Board.

Pre-Empt the Crash

EDITORIAL

Impose Glass-Steagall Now— Before Deutsche Bank Blow-Out

Oct. 3 (EIRNS)—There is not a moment to waste. Congress must be called back to Washington to immediately re-instate Glass Steagall—before the blowout of Deutsche Bank brings down the entire trans-Atlantic financial system and unleashes chaos and possible thermonuclear war on the planet.

As top executives from Deutsche Bank are in Washington, racing to cut a deal with the Justice Department to reduce the threatened $14 billion fine for mortgage securities fraud, it is now openly acknowledged that Deutsche Bank's overwhelming derivatives exposure and its 25:1 leverage is about to bring down the entire gambling casino of London and Wall Street. On Saturday, a judge in Milan, Italy, indicted six top current and former Deutsche Bank executives, along with 11 other top bankers from Banca Monte dei Paschi di Siena (BMPS) and Nomura, on charges they faked BMPS's books to conceal huge losses from regulators and customers. Russian prosecutors are investigating another former top Deutsche Bank broker from the bank's Moscow office, who was allegedly involved in a $10 billion money-laundering scheme with Russian mobsters.

While these prosecutions are going on, the U.S. Justice Department has yet to indict a single too-big-to-fail bank executive for the biggest financial fraud in history. As a result, an even bigger financial bubble, built upon hundreds of trillions of dollars in derivatives, has been built up again—and is now about to explode. A leading Japanese expert put it bluntly in a recent discussion: Either Glass-Steagall is re-instated before the blow-out, and all the top criminal bankers are arrested, or we all face the danger of a systemic crash and the threat of war. Echoing comments by Lyndon LaRouche, he declared "October is the critical moment."

Indeed, the only solution is the immediate re-instating of Glass Steagall, the termination of all of the derivatives contracts on a specific designated date, and the criminal prosecutions of all of the TBTF bankers who looted their own customers. The crimes recently uncovered at Wells Fargo are the actual norm within Wall Street and London. Don't forget the role of HSBC in laundering the cocaine proceeds from the Colombian and Mexican drug cartels, which financed their death squads.

The moment is ripe for just such emergency actions, followed immediately by the launching of a physical economic recovery, through world-scale capital investment in infrastructure, job creation, and scientific research. President Obama, the British, and the Saudis were just delivered the most devastating blow by the United States Congress, in overriding Obama's veto of JASTA. Obama, LaRouche observed to colleagues on Monday, is exhausted—his vitality is gone. Everything is collapsing around him, and he can and must be thoroughly boxed in so that he cannot do anything.

There is vitality in Asia, where the functioning of those leading nations—China, Russia, India, and others—must be defended against any desperate actions by Obama. The securing of the Asian initiatives, which will be advanced in 12 days when the BRICS heads of state gather in Goa, India, for their annual summit, is a global priority.

EIR Contents

www.larouchepub.com Volume 43, Number 41, October 7, 2016

Cover This Week

Francisco Osorio

Correction: The picture on page 16 of the Sept. 30, 2016 issue of *EIR* was published in error. It does not depict Deir al-Zour.

TO EDUCATE MANKIND MORE PROFOUNDLY

LaRouche in Dialogue: Revolutionize The *Idea* of Science!

In a discussion with leaders of his association on Sept. 30, Lyndon La-Rouche was single-minded and unflinching in his insistence that the crucial strategic issue today is the development of the human mind—and how that may be accomplished. Edited excerpts follow.

Lyndon LaRouche: Among the things that we have discussed in the preceding report today and earlier, there are some things that we have missed and which most people in our own organization rarely understand. The question in terms of economy involves not simply products capable of measurement as such, but rather involves the requirement of developing human minds in new ways that the human mind has even fashioned to do it. In other words, these are problems involved which cannot be explained; they have to be created. And without that, what we are trying to do here would be a failure, because the problem of mankind mainly is not what is complained about in usual political luster.

What is important is what makes human minds work. And there is very little attention to that question. There are certain things which are important, but the important thing now is we have to change the character of the craft of things. We are going to change things from what was being done up to now. And we are going to make a new start on the basis of understanding what are those principles—principles which almost no

Lyndon LaRouche

human being knows—and those principles which have to be included which have not been included up to the present time must be introduced. Otherwise, the attempt we are making will fail. And that, I think, is something we should probably take up right now. I think Jeff wants to talk about it as well. Let's continue from there.

Jeffrey Steinberg: I think that issue is obviously begged by the crisis moment that we have reached right now, in which the existing trajectory and directionality of things is doomed to fail. I think there are three situations that beg that issue, and put the question of a completely different approach and paradigm of thinking, starting from exactly that standpoint, of what is the nature of man and the question of how to create a system that drives this sort of human creativity.

Number one, it is very clear that the entire European banking situation, led by Deutsche Bank, is now at an absolute breaking point and that the perspective of just kicking the can down the road is not going to work. There is a very interesting statement quoted in *Bloomberg* today by a guy a guy named Michael Ingram of an outfit in London called BGC Partners. He said we have a very connected financial system, and a zombie financial system at some point translates into a zombie economy. He said that is exactly where we are headed. There is a *Marketwatch* piece that says Merkel is failing to respond properly to the Deutsche Bank crisis just as she has failed to respond to every crisis since she first came into office, and that this is now reaching a kind of existential moment. The *Wall Street Journal*'s story is headlined, "Deutsche Bank's Lehman Dilemma."

So they are basically saying we are potentially moments away from the entire financial system blowing out, and that there are many trigger spots in Europe, the lead one being obviously Deutsche Bank. They say that Merkel's continuing public insistence against any kind of intervention that would prevent the system from blowing out, is one of the greatest dangers at the moment. That's one issue, which is the imminent blowout and the unwillingness to take a creative approach.

The Power to Create New Sciences

LaRouche: But the most important thing, Jeff, is not what you just attested. What is important, which is *little known today*, is what is the power to create new sciences, new kinds of science, to bring the whole system of humanity into a functional form. Doing what you are talking about so far would not work. Therefore, that is what I'm emphasizing, that this would be an amateur night. It would be a nice amateur night, but it would be in effect an amateur night. Because mankind has not discovered the meaning of mankind. People want to talk about gimmicks, they want to talk about skills; those things are necessary in their own way, but they are not the creative force on which the existence of humanity depends. We have to mention that. Don't be practical. Stop being practical. Practical people are dead people.

What we have to do is develop the question of scientific thinking. For example, we have in the ocean and other places, areas which have a development process, almost like planets and so forth, and we have to change the character of everything in the universe. It has to be changed in one way or the other. That understanding is what has been destroyed! That is what has caused the fall. That is what has caused the crime—being practical, and as long as you operate on the basis of a practical system you will get a practical bunch of thieves, largely,

> "Mankind has not discovered the meaning of mankind. People want to talk about gimmicks, they want to talk about skills; those things are necessary in their own way, but they are not the creative force on which the existence of humanity depends."

and you will not understand what mankind's future is. And we have got to bring the question of what mankind's future is, what is mankind going to do that changes everything from what mankind has been doing up to now.

Few Understand the Problem

Diane Sare asks LaRouche if the optimism and future orientation of former Israeli Prime Minister Shimon Peres, recently deceased, is something we might want to address.

LaRouche: No. The important thing is the kind of thing that has not been understood heretofore. That is, technologies, approaches, space programs. The problem here is that people do not understand—most people on this planet do not understand—what that problem is, the problem of science, of real science, not of science as a copy of this, a copy of that, or something simple like that. This is what we have to do *now*; otherwise mankind cannot continue successfully the mission we just talked about. The mission is there, but the question is, what is the instrument which will make it work. And what we have discussed so far does not answer that problem.

In other words, all the things people suggest now, usually, in terms of recommendations, won't work, not for this purpose. You have got to recognize that the degeneration of the human mind, which has been induced over centuries, the degeneration of the human mind in most of the population of the world—that is the thing that prevents mankind from doing what we were talking about this morning. And we've got to change the subject. Don't get on that subject. We said that now. We are going to say it. But now we have to put in something else without which we will not succeed.

Do What Has Never Been Done Before

Sare reports that that night, John Sigerson will conduct the first seminar on the question of the scientific, Verdi tuning for the musicians and others who had participated in the series of performances of Mozart's Requiem, *as an escalation in developing their understanding of what is unique about our approach to the music, as opposed to the garbage and degeneration that typifies the New York music scene.*

LaRouche: I'll make two points on this. First of all, what John will do, because I know John, and I know how his mind works, at least fairly well, I don't know everything that goes on in his mind, but I do know him and I've worked with him and we've worked together. The idea of classical music composition the way John would deal with it, when presented, represents one part, a very significant part, but a peculiar part of what we have to do to create a discovery of the ability of the human population to actually be successful.

Now the issue here is being successful. Not successful in getting money or this or that, but successful in achieving *what has never been done before!* And John is in a category of those who can comment on that and develop that idea in very important aspects quite readily. I would point out the importance of his work on that account. But the point is, don't try to give a simplification. I'm talking about something that most of you here don't know yet.

What I'm talking about is what you don't know. And that is what has to be delivered. You will get it on islands, for example, or the Moon, or the [Moon's dark side]. You'll find out that things are there which force mankind to consider new things which have to be done. But the usual thing of practical development of economy will not work. The population is not ready to handle it.

Mankind Stupefied by Its Cultures

Steinberg: You mentioned yesterday, Lyn, that you had some thoughts on reviving a lot of the basement work …

LaRouche: No, I'm not. I'm talking about science, not basement. Most people don't know it. We have some people who have the elements of the ability—like John's case. John Sigerson has a plan. I understand what the plan is. I don't know the details of what he knows, but I know John. I know his mind, and that's important. It contains something which is unique. It is not something you can copy. And the same thing is true of everything else. The broad length is we are going to have to explore space. We are going to largely explore space. It is one of the most important issues to be taken up immediately! Don't get into something else and say this will do it, that will do it. It will not do it.

The point is that mankind has been stupefied by its economy, its economies, its cultures, the cultures and forms of skills of mankind have been largely stupid, stupidity of one kind or another. Now the time has come when we have to approach not only the immediate things we can point out, but we've got to concentrate on real science, not what is called science, but real science. Without real science we cannot make it.

The Galactic Perspective

Benjamin Deniston: I think one of the frontiers is the galactic perspective …

LaRouche: Of course! The inability to present a competent study of what the galactic system means—when you include some of the space program objectives—there you begin to get into science. You get into science then and only then, and into the real sociology of the human mind. And that is what we've got to do now. We cannot go back to some new version of an old thing. We have to realize that what has been done in the past by some of the greatest minds, that have been rare minds, have developed this kind of process.

The practical man—most people are practical men and women—is not scientific in terms of any real science. They call themselves scientists because they have a scientific label. But they are not really scientists. Einstein was a scientist, and Einstein knew that you cannot have a mathematical conclusion. And that is an example of what the problem is. Einstein did not ever make himself a practical man. He investigated the effect—what the role of mankind is in space, in the universe. A lot of people who admire Einstein don't know that. They think they've got some practical thing they can use. It doesn't work. But if you look at it from the Einstein side, the actual Einstein side, you are getting into the right area.

You're going to move planets! You're going to move everything! You're going to have to change the rules of planetary existence. These things have to be done quickly. We can improvise for a short period of time, but the foundation of our campaign has to be more profound.

> "Mankind has been stupefied by its economies, its cultures, … Now the time has come when we have to approach not only the immediate things, but we've got to concentrate on real science. Without real science we cannot make it."

Understanding the galactic system: "there you begin to get into science." Here, our Galaxy, the Milky Way, as we see it from our place in the galactic disk.

The Einstein Principle

Deniston: I really think this Einstein reference that you have developed, or the Einstein principle, really, is critical, because if you are talking about the Galaxy or really understanding the Solar system, it's an issue of new principles. It's not just derivations or descriptions ...

LaRouche: Exactly! You've got it! It's what we've learned from Einstein: After what we think we've learned from his experimental work, we find out there's another layer beyond that, and that is the discovery of what the meaning of science is. And Einstein was unique in that respect. Many people thought they had understood Einstein on the basis of this or that theory, but that's an amateur issue. The more profound thing—and the aspect of Einstein that is more profound than practically anybody else who's working in science—is to understand this: You have to understand that what mankind has to change, are the principles of science, the principles of the practice of science, from a Solar way. And that is what mankind is going to rely upon to save our civilization from what we are trying to fight against now.

We've got to educate mankind in a more profound way than most people have imagined. And you're going to have to educate them, and you're going to have to find ways to do it. I think as a case in space managed under China, under China's science, that would be a good starting point.

Living in the Future

Kesha Rogers: What came to mind is the question of the mind of Einstein, or take Krafft Ehricke, as living in the future. I was reminded of Ehricke's 1966 article, in which he wrote as if he were in 2001, looking back on 1966—the question of space travel and development of space from the standpoint of living in that future that you are already hoping to create, that you are already destined to create. Not just going from some kind of bottom-up perspective, but starting from what is man's rightful place in the Universe, what is man's rightful place in the Galaxy.

That is the way China is thinking. They have already committed themselves to that higher identity of mankind—not just going to the Moon and then taking the next step and traveling out into space. They have already defined what the potential of mankind is in terms of our destiny and our role in developing and conquering space in the way that Krafft Ehricke understood.

LaRouche: Exactly! Exactly so! And this is the same thing as his science prospect. Everything that we need as human beings, everything we need is exactly what I'm talking about. Don't try to change it back to something more conventional. You just screw things up.

What we have to do now is something previously considered impossible. The most advanced work of Einstein, which is not what many people think, as a practical thing, but what Einstein did with his mind was precisely in that direction, of how mankind can develop mankind. What we're talking about in this whole issue here, if you want to develop mankind, you've got to go by the right rules, and you cannot do it by practical methods. We can do it. We can do it right now under these conditions. We can do it in certain parts of the world. We've got to do it. But we've got to be discretionary. Don't be practical! It will make you all fools, as before.

Anyway, that's my point, and I think that is a concluding point on the argument of principle, and I think anything else would be a fallacy in practice, under these kinds of conditions. We want to get out of this, what the past has done to us; we've got to go by the path of the future.

Flanking the Enemy

Rogers: I think it is beautiful, because you always find that the enemy of mankind tries to set the terms of what is allowed, or what is going to be the determining factor in the discussion. Instead of playing by what they say, we must outflank them with something more profound, a higher conception. What you just presented is a real flank against the enemy, the enemy of the creative process, whose real target is the creative identity of the human mind.

We are looking at devastation in the world now—the murders, the war threat, the attacks against China, the fact that we are at the brink of total annihilation—so you start to think about how you address those things from a lower level. But what you just presented is that they are out to destroy the souls and the minds of the human species, and if you want to take them on on that, there is no other approach than what you have just presented.

LaRouche: Yep.

Revolutionize the *Idea* of Science

Steinberg: It reminds me that when Deng Xiaoping came to power in the late seventies, early eighties, he said don't give me any titles, don't give me any mundane responsibilities. My first priority is building up the scientific capacity of China. He said if we can focus and concentrate our effort on reviving science and training

> "The aspect of Einstein that is more profound than practically anybody else who's working in science—is to understand this: You have to understand that what mankind has to change, is the principles of science, the principles of the practice of science… And that is what mankind is going to rely upon to save our civilization from what we are trying to fight against now."

a generation of new scientists and engineers who think that way, then China will emerge in thirty years as a great nation, leading the world in this area.

LaRouche: That has the smack of being practical, but I don't think so. What I am thinking about is something much more important. The point is you've got to get at this and realize you've got to revolutionize the *idea* of science, not revolutionize this or that. You've got to emphasize the revolution of the *idea of science*. That's where we've lost. That's where the United States, Europe, and so forth have lost. There are some parts of the world where we have just had an example of this, of studying things of a higher order. But practical things, or things which have a practical nature, will not get us out of what we've been into recently. It will fail, as mankind's practice has failed before, because *that* science does not really understand science.

So why don't we just go on and get into this science business. Present the question of what are the issues of *a higher science for mankind now!* That is what you've got to concentrate on. Don't think about knicks and knacks. You've got to make a revolution in technology, right now. That means scientific technology, not practical technology.

The Back of the Moon

After interrupting an intelligence briefing, LaRouche returns to his main theme.

LaRouche: China has been developing a program to study the far side of the Moon. It is something which has been done before in a certain way, but it is very important. This aspect of exploration is probably the best spiritual source to get people to understand what these methods are. Don't try to say you are going to discover the method. You've got to say what they are, what do they do.

You look into space, and find we have a situation where we do have a Moon, which we don't know yet how to deal with entirely, a large Moon, and it is that kind of mentality which has to be focussed on, and it has to be specified on that basis. Not something like, well maybe we can get there. We have got to get there now. This is the kind of thing that can enable us to move the population into new areas, the kind of new areas where they will discover the ability to think. Right now most people in society do not have the power to think. Not really. The human being is capable of thinking, but you've got to make it happen.

Tease the Imagination

LaRouche again interrupts an intelligence update, and continues.

This does not go the point I am raising. What I'm saying now is generally not understood by most people. The question is, what is the existing scientific potential on which the future of mankind depends, not some gimmick. We've got to educate the people, young people, we've got to train them. We've got to do all the kinds of things which will tease the imagination of the young student. That is the way, by feeding that question, as I know from my experience. That question is the way you get to real science. And you get into the kind of things that allow us

> The question is, what is the existing scientific potential on which the future of mankind depends, not some gimmick. We've got to educate the people, young people... We've got to do all the kinds of things which will tease the imagination of the young student. That is the way you get to real science.

to get back to what we've lost, over the lifespan of most people on the planet.

They've lost it! We've got to give them back the means of regaining what they've lost. Otherwise the whole thing will fail. We want science! We want absolute science! We want space science. We want the kinds of things that grab the imagination and produce the people who become recruited to that kind of work. Without that we lose.

Remember how bad this planet has been in terms of its behavior. Just think of every part of the planet—nation after nation after nation. What have you got? You've got some people who have good intentions. You've got some people who achieve things. But in main, the human species has failed. And we've got to do something about that right now, or begin right from there. I think we can explore the Moon, which is what China is doing. That would be a good starting point, to get at what is the problem and how do we approach it.

Everything else will follow.

Congress Delivers a Deafening Blow To Obama and the Anglo-Saudis

by Jeffrey Steinberg

Oct. 2 (EIRNS)—Congress on Thursday, Sept. 29 resoundingly overrode President Barack Obama's Sept. 23 veto of S-2040, the Justice Against Sponsors of Terrorism Act (JASTA). The Senate vote tally was 97-to-1, in favor of override; and the House of Representatives tally was 348-to-77. The override required a 2/3 majority vote in both Houses of Congress, and it was achieved by a wide, bipartisan margin.

The implications are profound and far-reaching.

With JASTA now the law of the land, the loopholes that blocked the 9/11 survivors and families from suing the Kingdom of Saudi Arabia in U.S. Federal Court for its complicity in 9/11 have now been removed. A hearing is already scheduled in Federal Court for the Southern District of New York on Oct. 20, at which the 9/11 families will be able to finally begin to directly confront the Saudi Monarchy and pursue further evidence of the Saudi government support for the 9/11 hijackers, 15 of whom were Saudi citizens.

But beyond the profound issues surrounding the Sept. 11, 2001 attacks and the growth of Saudi-sponsored Wahhabi/Salafi terrorism, the message from the Congress must now radiate out to other existential issues threatening the United States, starting with the urgent, immediate need to restore the Glass-Steagall Act, which separated commercial and investment banking, and the launching of a genuine economic recovery in the United States.

The dramatic break with the Obama policy of protecting the Saudis and covering up the true authorship of 9/11 means that, with the proper mobilization of the American people, Congress can be compelled to take

videograb from BBC Panorama show

Saudi Prince Bandar and British Prime Minister Margaret Thatcher.

the other actions that mean the difference between the survival and destruction of the United States and much of the rest of the world.

The Saudi 9/11 Case

The opportunity for discovery about the Saudi role in the Sept. 11, 2001, attacks was recently further enhanced by the public release, on July 15, 2016, of the 28-page chapter from the original 2002 Joint Congressional Inquiry into 9/11, which revealed previously secret evidence about the role of former Saudi Ambassador to the United States Prince Bandar bin Sultan in supporting at least two of the 9/11 terrorists, along with evidence of ties to the hijackers by scores of other Saudi officials at all levels of government and the Royal Family.

The role of Prince Bandar in the 9/11 attacks is of special significance because of his close ties to the Bush family and even closer ties to the British. Bandar was the broker, along with former British Prime Minister Margaret Thatcher, of the Al-Yamamah deal, a barter arrangement of British weapons for Saudi oil. Under Al-Yamamah, hundreds of billions of dollars were squirreled into secret off-shore joint Anglo-Saudi accounts for the purpose of funding terrorism, asassinations, and political coups around the globe. A prominent Member of the British House of Commons, who is also a senior figure in the British defense establishment, candidly warned in June that, if JASTA were to become U.S. law, the British Monarchy and the British government could be sued, along with the Saudis.

'An Historic Victory'

Lyndon LaRouche, whose LaRouche Political Action Committee (LPAC) had mobilized intensively for the Sept. 29 results, described the vote as "An historic victory. It is a cause for rejoicing; it has turned the pages of history. The worldwide positive potential is enormous." However, LaRouche cautioned, "How far and where it takes us, is not yet clear. Get ready to find out." He added, "Remember, you've hurt the devil hard. And the devil ain't going to thank you for that!"

On Saturday, Oct. 1, LaRouche addressed the weekly meeting of the Manhattan LPAC activists, and made clear the strategic significance of the JASTA vote. He told the activists that "we have just won a great victory already, even in the short-term presently; because what you saw in the Congress in that one vote, which humiliated Obama, we had won the battle. We had not just won the battle for the United States, or part of the United States. What we have gained is a new view of first of all, the European area; the European area is now ready to be trained and developed. What's happened in Asia is, Asia is now the center of the whole development of mankind at this time. This is going to lead to investment in the skies and the islands out there; this is going to reach out throughout the Solar System and beyond."

The overwhelming defeat of President Obama and the Saudis came despite the fact that the entire Obama Administration had been mobilized to pressure Congress to support his veto, and the Saudi Monarchy had poured in a reported $9.4 million, in a desperate lobbying effort to buy off Members of Congress. In the end, a bipartisan coalition of leading Senators and Representatives rejected the Obama Administration lies that

White House/Pete Souza
Senate Minority Leader Harry Reid (D-Nev.), left, conferring with President Obama before a 2010 appearance in Nevada.

JASTA posed a threat to American interests abroad, and delivered the biggest political defeat to President Obama since he first took office.

Obama's Personal Intervention

On the eve of the vote, President Obama sent a personal message to the leaders of both Houses of Congress, imploring them not to override his veto. Senate Minority Leader Harry Reid (D-Nev.) read President Obama's letter to all of the Senate Democrats, according to one eyewitness account—and the only vote that was swayed by the personal appeal was that of Harry Reid. Every other Democrat and every Republican voted to repudiate the President, in the most profound repudiation of Obama or any recent president in memory.

On Sept. 29, each House of Congress engaged in two hours of debate, preceding the historic vote, and the vast majority of speeches emphasized the rights of the 9/11 families to at long last obtain justice, and to confront the Saudi Monarchy and its agents for their complicity in the worst terrorist attack to ever occur on U.S. soil.

Much of the debate was taken up debunking the Obama claim that JASTA would open American servicemen, corporations and diplomats to retaliation by foreign governments. Leading JASTA proponents, including Senators Charles Grassley (R-Iowa) and

Charles Schumer (D-New York), and Representatives Robert Goodlatte (R-Va.) and Jerome Nadler (D-New York) made clear, repeatedly, that JASTA merely closes a loophole in legislation that has existed since the 1970s, which had not allowed American citizens to sue foreign governments proven to have provided support for terrorist attacks that took place on U.S. soil. Under the previous version of the law, payments to terrorists that took place outside the United States were not sufficient to waive sovereign immunity. That loophole allowed the Kingdom of Saudi Arabia to evade American justice for the past 15 years—and that has now come to an end.

Broader Strategic Opportunities

The successful bipartisan effort, beating President Obama's veto of JASTA, can and must now be directed, with equal intensity, at other vital issues, starting with the need for Congress to immediately pass the bills already before both Houses of Congress to reinstate the Glass-Steagall Act, to break up the too-big-to-fail banks that are on the edge of a collapse far worse than 2008. Germany's Deutsche Bank, reportedly the largest holder of derivatives of any bank in the world, is about to collapse, and the entire trans-Atlantic banking system is set to crash, as the direct result.

Reinstating Glass-Steagall is the indispensable first step towards launching a genuine economic recovery through massive capital investment in urgently needed infrastructure projects, research and development, and particularly a revival of America's now collapsed NASA space program. Such an effort, now, can create millions of new productive jobs. In Eurasia, under the leadership of China, a tremendous program of infrastructure investment is being implemented, under the banner of President Xi Jinping's One Belt, One Road initiative. Russian President Vladimir Putin has embraced the initiative and has proposed to integrate the Eurasian Economic Union into the effort, which former U.S. Ambassador Chas Freeman recently described as the biggest infrastructure project in human history.

Rather than working to sabotage the New Silk Road project—which has been the U.S. policy under President Obama—the United States should fully embrace the One Belt, One Road program and thus expand it into a true World Land-Bridge.

The U.S. Congress, for the first time in a long time, has acted with a single voice, on behalf of the vital interests of the American people. JASTA benefits all Americans and particularly those who lost loved ones in the 9/11 attacks or were themselves severely injured.

That vote offers a larger beacon of hope, that the same spirit of national interest can now rapidly be translated into the other actions, that are vital to the survival and prosperity of the United States and the world.

Champions Needed

The enduring lesson of the strategic victory in releasing the 28 pages and passing JASTA is that a small number of Members of Congress who step forward to take a leadership role can make a decisive difference. In the case of 9/11, and in the case of Glass Steagall, there is a large and growing public constituency for taking bold action. But they require a champion, to take up the fight regardless of the consequences. That was the all-or-nothing approach taken by Rep. Walter Jones (R-NC) with respect to the 28 pages and JASTA. Such a champion is vitally needed for the fight to restore Glass-Steagall and start the process of genuine economic recovery.

Signing on as a cosponsor is not enough. What have you done to actually force it through and make it law? What will you do today?

Let's Begin the Renaissance of Creativity in Manhattan

This is an edited transcript of Lyndon LaRouche's dialogue with the Manhattan Project, Oct. 1, 2016.

Dennis Speed: On behalf of the LaRouche Political Action Committee, I want to welcome you here today, October 1st, for a dialogue with Lyndon LaRouche himself. We're really happy that Lyn is with us to do this. It was a victory this week in the Congress; humanity showed up. But Lyn has been insisting that we do something a bit more than just show up. We want you to keep your questions short and focussed, leaving as much time as possible for the answers. So, we're going to go right to it. Lyn, do you have an opening statement for us, or do we just go right to questions and answers?

Lyndon LaRouche: I have one thing which is quite functionally necessary. We've gone through things here in Manhattan; what we've celebrated here. And we have rejoiced also here on the relevant occasions. We hope that we will do more of that; and I'm confident that we should be able to do more of that. So, that's where we start, and let's go into it.

Speed: OK, great.

A Revolution in the Idea of Science

Elliot Greenspan: We're continuing that process as we speak. Today is China National Day, and we've got a good number of our choristers who are participating in that celebration with a huge concert—about eleven different choruses in Flushing, New York. We are the only mixed chorus; that is, all the other choruses are Chinese, our chorus is mixed. But this comes in the context of the series of developments from the beginning of September. You have often referenced Percy Shelley's "In Defence of Poetry," and Shelley's emphasis that there are moments in history in which the capacity for humanity to receive and impart profound and impassioned conceptions respecting Man and Nature is enhanced. What we saw around 9/11, with the series of Mozart *Requiem* concerts, what we saw then with the successful fight to defeat Obama on JASTA, this was all in the context of what happened in Asia at the beginning of the month with the summit of the Group of 20, [and then the East Asian Economic Forum in Vladivostok, and the ASEAN meeting in Vientane]. This is a very profound historic transformation, and we are very much central to it.

Yesterday, I found what you did in a Policy Committee discussion and what then ensued with the webcast, and what John Sigerson then did in the evening with a class here on the science of music, the science of tuning; I found this extremely striking and valuable. In the LaRouche PAC daily lead, which many of the people here might have read this morning, which went

Lyndon H. LaRouche, Jr.

LPAC

out across the nation this morning, it begins from LaRouche: "We need a revolution in the idea of science to survive." And it says at the outset: "In discussion today with the Policy Committee, the Basement, and others, Lyndon LaRouche declared that unless we can develop the minds of human beings in new ways by making new discoveries of scientific principles, we will not survive." I would be very appreciative if you could elaborate on the import of that, what you were working with yesterday. It seems to me there's a dramatic relationship between these developments of the prior weeks—of the Mozart *Requiem*, of our victory here, and so on—and your looking toward a higher order for the future.

LaRouche: Well, we've got a good deal of it in the United States, in certain quarters of the United States in particular. We have a bunch of people who voted for this victory [Congress' override of Obama's veto of JASTA], and they're there. Other people have also been available there in the course of things. We have people who have been missed, who didn't turn their votes in, in time; but we'll fix that, and we have the power to fix it. Because what we've done in the Congress and elsewhere, we have won the cause against Obama; we won it! Now we have to do some more winning, because some of the people who were here and could have been involved, didn't show up that way. So, we're going to have to have a mass movement re-emphasized again. And right from there, where you're standing right now, is one of those key points where the developments have to spin out quickly.

The JASTA Override: 'Your Cue to Win'

Renee Sigerson: Hi there Lyn; just want to say "Hello," and it's wonderful to see you. Without getting overly preoccupied with what has happened in the past, I have to say that I wanted to share this with you, that what occurred on the day of the slamming or shutting of Obama into the trap of his own making, really had a certain character to it. A very eerie character, reminiscent of the greatest classical drama. We were watching this step by step in the office, and it was really gripping to watch the empty room echoing with what one person subsequently said was like the ghost of Banquo roaming around in that empty chamber, where one by one these individuals were getting up—these Senators—and presenting their case.

The greatest shock for me personally was Cornyn. I never thought in my life that I would ever be gripped by a statement from a right-wing Texas Senator; frankly, I thought Cornyn did a fantastic job. He not only presented the case very succinctly and personally, but he then proceeded to make an ironical reference to the British monarchy, which he just left hanging, resonating in the chamber there. It really caused me to think about how these great earthquakes in history sometimes occur in this very eerie fashion; but the mistake would be to think that the venue will always be the same.

In other words, to think that simply by repeating what we did with Congress with another subject, will produce the same effect. He was just talking about a mass movement, and it seems to me that that's really exactly the point. As in the *Requiem* concert and other places where we did this, there's got to be an engagement that these guys are responding to—not just to what

---

LaRouche on Laughter, Music, and Creativity

From a memorandum with this title, originally written by LaRouche in June 1976, privately circulated to his philosophical associates at that time, and published in EIR, *Jan. 4, 1991:*

Although ultimately it is the lawful order of the universe as a whole which determines what is and what is not a solution to a problem, the form in which the problem is posed is the set of rules representing the best approximation of universal knowledge. The immediate characteristic of most problem-solving is a solution to a problem which satisfies existing *laws of scientific knowledge*.

More rarely, more profoundly, there are crucial discoveries which redefine and add to the previously existing bodies of lawful scientific knowledge. It is the location of freedom (creative innovation) within a determining set of lawful knowledge of reality which is the first-approximation definition of creative work. However, that is not adequate by itself. *Random*, impulsive alterations in behavior (*freedom* as the anarchists and other lunatics misdefine the term) is not creative problem-solving. Man's successful mastery of the universe, is the criterion—and active content—of creative work, *of creative mental activity as such*.

---

was going on in that room; they're responding to what they know is beginning to erupt across the country. Can you say more about that?

LaRouche: I would say the same thing; people are ready to fill themselves with joy, and to enjoy the expression of that matter. The point is, what's happened is obvious. Members of Congress have all said things that meant they were jumping in the way that they did; the way they responded. We had a victory, which came from the center of Manhattan; it was Manhattan which radiated this idea of authority. And that's what made this thing work; and it made the Congress work, and it made Obama dead. [laughter]

Sigerson: [follow-up] Oh, by the way, it's unbelievable: This guy is so out of his mind that in the last 24 hours, he gave a speech in memory of Shimon Peres and tried to honor him by comparing him to Empress Elizabeth. This guy is really completely off his rocker.

LaRouche: He's defective; we all know that.

Albert Einstein, 1931: "The most beautiful thing we can experience is the mysterious. It is the source of all true art and all science. He to whom this emotion is a stranger, who can no longer pause to wonder and stand rapt in awe, is as good as dead: his eyes are closed."

Galipedia

Ian Brinkley: Hi, Lyn; Ian Brinkley here from Boston. I was thinking about the passage of JASTA and the implications of this; and my mind started to wander to the period immediately preceding the close of World War II, when Allied troops were moving across Germany and discovering the concentration camps. And the way in which the Allied forces would go to the German towns and take people and walk them through the camps, to show them what they had accepted from their government, what kind of genocide and fraud and evil they had tolerated as a people. And it seems to me that we're at a point now where that's the only historical example that I can think of that's comparable to the kind of self-discovery process which the American people are going to have to undergo now when it is revealed how members of our government have been involved in mass murder, including 9/11.

LaRouche: Well, I would say we have just won a great victory already, even in the short-term; because what you saw in the Congress in that one vote which humiliated Obama, we had won the battle. We had not just won the battle for the United States, or part of the United States. What we have gained is a new view of, first of all, the European area; the European area is now ready to be trained and developed. What's happened in Asia is, Asia is now the center of the whole development of mankind at this time. This is going to lead to investment in the skies and the islands out there; this is going to reach out throughout the Solar System and beyond.

Question: Good afternoon, Mr. LaRouche, it's great to see you. First, I would like to honor you for your brilliant leadership creating a profound future for the world. Last Tuesday, I had the pleasure of joining Terry Strada and the 9/11 Families in Washington, D.C. All I can say is, the impact was felt all around the world. I'm in the process of organizing a concert at an Italian center in my hometown in Connecticut. Verdi will be appropriate.

Question: Hi, Mr. LaRouche, this is Rick from Bergen County, New Jersey. I've been thinking about the passage of the JASTA bill, and I've been thinking about some of the deeper implications down the road of what it means from the point of view of humanism. I don't want to go into any detail here, but I see it as a very far-reaching piece of legislation that will hopefully cause certain entities that have been destroying people, destroying their property, destroying them physically, a very large number of people numbering in the hundreds of millions who were killed by nations in the 20th Century and we still have it happening today,— I see JASTA as a way of getting back and having people protect themselves against this type of activity.

I have a list of names of 78 people, and my question to you is, these are people who did not vote to override the veto. I see that as an act of—it's un-American, it's treachery, it's anti-patriotic. My question to you is, what do you think should be done with such individuals who, in my opinion, shouldn't be in office? And in my opinion, their passports should be revoked; because I don't consider them to be U.S. citizens.

LaRouche: There are some considerations for that kind of thing; but I think the essential thing is to concentrate on what the Congress did in that landslide, where one person of the wrong class actually survived. The problem is now, we've got to take what we can do with our own United States; get our own United States population put into order. Use the experience that we reached in that event; use that to remind yourself of what *we*, the people of the United States, can do of their own will, as they did in that override. And that's it. We've got to fight some enemies, there's no question about that; that's a fact. And that lesson from the way the Congress voted in that one case, that's your cue to win.

'You Electrified the Mobilization'

Speed: Lyn, I want to come to the microphone at this point, because I want to ask you something. It will help, because last week we had our meeting here; you observed it. You had some very sharp things to say. The next day, the whole mobilization changed. That's just what happened. Elliot in particular took a very specific role; there was a drive. Everybody was either in the office, or wherever they were,— suddenly, every minute that passed, people were *all focussed* on getting the objective that you had defined.

LaRouche: Very simple. I had a cause to do. And I was gripping on this thing; I was not being cautious, I was gripping on this.

LPAC

LaRouche PAC organizer after Obama's veto of the JASTA bill.

Speed: Yes, and that's what the difference was. And you've seen this whole process in Manhattan, I would argue, at least a little bit differently than many of us. We've been doing it, we've been organizing it; but you see something that at least I believe I haven't seen at various times. So I'm asking you, we got the victory and you made the point that this shows what we can do.

LaRouche: Yes, but what we can do is in the fact that Wall Street has lost the war. Now they haven't declared that; but they have lost the power of money, and it's going to be fully taken away from them in due course. So therefore, that's the way we ought to look at this. We are going to take their dollars and so forth away; not to take anything that they own, but to prevent them from wasting our money.

Organize for Victory

Question: Good afternoon Lyn; how are you today?

LaRouche: Oh, I'm fairly well, considering my condition.

Question: This question is focussed around China's role in the world right now. It's a statement also. As you know, I was just in China some three or four months ago, and through my cultural education while I was there, I found out—not only from lecturers, but from the youth themselves—that they are raised to believe that it is their given duty to bring the world together, through self-reflection, through discovery, through culture, through morality. And they've been at this mission for centuries now; it's not something that just has come up, it's something that they've been at for a long time. From when they sent out envoys across the world, and said, "Here's our technology. Here's our goods, here's our services; here's what we have to offer. What do you have to offer?" They've been at this for a very long time.

Also, on the other hand, I found out that they're all raised to be apolitical, which is not necessarily a bad thing. It's "Don't get caught up in the word of the day; don't get caught up in the politics of the situation. Get caught up in what you can do for the future and now."

LaRouche: Well, I'm not too much concerned about that, because what had happened is, the government of China has done a pretty good job in leadership and building up this kind of process; so you don't have to do much about that. There are other parts of Eurasia—nearby Eurasia—which have to be fixed up a little bit. But I think China, Russia, and some other locations will be the building center for the reconstruction of the entire region, for the entire world. What we're going to have to do is just remind people that that's the job, and to encourage them to leap into the task. We've got to realize we're dealing with space, just like one of our great heroes did, in starting up the space program. But the space program, as done at that time, is really the key to what we have to do on a global scale—not just national. Global. And it's going to come fast.

Question: Hi, Lyndon LaRouche; my name is C—, and it's an honor to speak to you and see you. I have noticed, time and time again, the majority of Americans are reluctant to learn or realize what is happening in our country. People are eager to keep up with celebrity news instead of the future of our country. Many dedicate their time to watching football and wondering who will win the next championship. We have become a culture obsessed with celebrities and have given up hope on beating the system. Many have forgotten their rights, and act as if those who speak truth are conspiracy theorists. The average American does not care what is happening or keep up with the news. We live in a society that accepts double standards without realizing it. How can we encourage people to make a difference? What will it take for people to stop being preoccupied with entertainment?

LaRouche: Look at that Congressional agreement and the remarkable thing that happened, where only one member of the Senate balked on supporting it. The entire body of the Congress supported this revolution. Obama was wiped out politically; he was wiped out on that occasion politically. And the seeds for that kind of correction happened in nearby areas like New Jersey and so forth. The point is, we are on the road to the way to victory; we simply have to get ourselves organized to make sure we are actually being organized for victory.

Agapē and Truth

John Sigerson: Hi, Lyn. Thinking about this seemingly unbelievable miracle that occurred in Congress, it seems to me there were two important elements that made this work. One was *agapē*, selfless Christian love for those victims of 9/11 and the love for the families. The second ingredient was truth. They were backed morally into a corner; even people who—probably despite themselves—were backed into a corner because of these two elements that they just could not wiggle themselves out of in any moral fashion whatsoever. This brings me to the other part of my comment and question, which has to do with Mozart.

For some reason—and it's almost a miracle—Mozart's music, almost uniquely, if done properly, is able to emanate that quality of *agapē*. Yesterday, I gave a class in which I attempted to elaborate this from the standpoint of your breakthroughs all the way back in your early days in 1948-52, your breakthroughs in both music and culture and economics. And I tried to weave those two together for many musicians who really have not thought these things through yet. One thing that struck me was your preoccupation all the way back then with the Mozart Fantasy, K. 475. If you have anything to say about what intrigued you so much, and what bothered you so much about that particular piece from the standpoint of Mozart's significance for *agapē*, I'd love you to say something.

LaRouche: It was death, an ugly death which was

planted on him deliberately to kill him and to bury him in a pauper's grave, almost unknown. And here's one of the greatest minds in all of modern history; and therefore, what people can understand in Mozart's orchestrations, when they can understand what the value is and capture the effect that Mozart gave in his lifetime for music, then you have something which is really precious. This is something that for Beethoven,— Mozart is a part of Beethoven, and so forth. The whole history of modern music is based on Mozart.

And we've done fairly well in some cases actually, in the practice of Mozart's work. I think if you want to do something about it in that way, just make sure that you do it up to date in fixing some of our Mozart work. And that will do the job. You can't explain it; you have to hear it. [laughter]

Deutsche Bank and Glass-Steagall

Question: On a different topic, this is Rick from Bergen County, New Jersey. Deutsche Bank is getting more prominently in the news; I'm seeing articles about the drop in their stock price, which is only 4 points, but on a percentage basis is down from something like 15 to 11.50 over the last few days. People are starting to talk about moving their accounts to other banks, and hedge funds are selling their investments. There's a pending $14 billion settlement with the U.S. government due to abuses in mortgage-backed securities markets, manipulating LIBOR, and who knows what else.

So it seems to me that this is a company that's about to go under. You addressed this issue quite a while ago. Given that you are there now, have you been focussing on this issue? And do you think we should use it as a leverage point to create concern in Congress so that they will be moved to pass Glass-Steagall?

LaRouche: Well, it's going to take more than that. It will take more than the German situation to do it. The principle lies there. It does exist. It can be developed. We look for times when we hope that certain members of Congress would disappear, maybe [German Finance Minister] Schäuble, and so forth—they would disappear. That would be a blessing to all mankind. We may not get that particular one. But we have neighboring areas, which are willing—because they're tied to China, to Russia, and so forth—to do what has to be done. So that one way or other, what has to be done in Europe can be done, and it should be done, right now.

Daniel Burke: Hi Lyn! It's Daniel here.

LaRouche: I see you're elevated again. [laughs]

Burke: We listened carefully to what you said yesterday with the Policy Committee about the worst misconceptions that people have about economics and about the meaning of science. I'm dying to hear more from you about this, particularly what the relationship is between mankind and the Galaxy.

LaRouche: It's the forced development within nations which leads them to build their own succor, and that's what we have to do. We have to understand that we are responsible for other nations; which ones and how they are to be treated, that's a big matter of discussion. But we have to have a conception that nations, as nations, must be brought together in comradeship.

A Profound Change Within Reach

Speed: Mr. Ingraham? We have a visitor here, Lyn.

Bob Ingraham: Hi Lyn! This is Bob Ingraham. Elliot, basically, forced me to get up. [laughter] Earlier today I visited Alexander Hamilton's home. It's called The Grange. It's here in Manhattan, at 141st Street in West Harlem. It was surprisingly interesting—the exhibits. One of the things that struck me was the short period of time—through a quality of personal morality and commitment—in which a revolutionary change was accomplished, by Hamilton and others.

My question to you—I don't want to give a long story here—my question is this: Often people get demoralized and depressed by a lot of things—the population, the culture, Congress, you name it. But it strikes me that we're at a moment right now where we have within our reach—it's almost tangible—the realization, not just the potential, but the real possibility of a *profound* change in the future of mankind; that this is right here. If you look at the implications of this vote on JASTA, if you look at Deutsche Bank and the collapse of the financial system, and if you look at what China and Russia are doing, and the position of strength they're in, whether or not everything they're doing is perfect . . .

Because people look at Hillary Clinton and Donald Trump, and they say, "Oh my God! There's not going to be any leadership for the country." But I think that it doesn't matter who gets elected, or what these guys think they're going to do. That through the intervention that is being made by us, by you, by Putin, by China, and everything else—the Chinese program to the Moon, the space program—we are *very, very close*, as in the time of Dante Alighieri or Filippo Brunelleschi, we are very close to a *profound* change in the future direction of society. This is in front of us, if we work for it.

LaRouche: We had a time when we created the space program. It was done right after right after World War II. It was done by great leaders. One of these leaders died because he had a disease, which prevented him from continuing. His death caused, largely, the condition which broke up the possibilities of the great cultural freedom that was given to us. Part of this [break-up] was done because of malice, part of it was done by Obama. Obama was one of the biggest factors that ever walked down the street, to kill the nation of the United States.

But this being the case, we've come into a time when we do have the option of developing, soon, and rapidly, the kind of revolution which had been desired before, after World War II. And now we're going to go in the same direction, freshly, to do the same thing. We have to bring a change in the development of the program of the people. We have to get something moving, moving in that real way. And we can do it.

Just look at one thing. What happened in the Congress? What happened with the override of Obama's veto of JASTA in the Congress? It was a miracle! Well, we can get more miracles. [applause]

An Arc from the Concerts to JASTA

Maria Channon: Hi Lyn! I just wanted to follow up on what John was saying earlier. I've been thinking a lot about this process from the concerts to this victory with JASTA. I have to say that in calling the victory a "miracle," I think you really put it precisely, because when you go through a transformation like that, it's life-changing. I think what John identified, that there

Friedrich Schiller, 1788:
"In the case of the creative mind, it seems to me, the intellect has withdrawn its watchers from the gates, and the ideas rush in pell-mell, and only then does it review and inspect the multitude. You worthy critics, or whatever you may call yourselves, are ashamed or afraid of the momentary and passing madness which is found in all real creators, the longer or shorter duration of which distinguishes the thinking artist from the dreamer. Hence your complaints of unfruitfulness, for you reject too soon and discriminate too severely." Einstein intersected this idea when he wrote: "Man only plays when he is in the fullest sense of the word a human being, and he is only fully a human being when he plays."

Public domain

were two elements at play—*agapē* and truth—I was going to say it was a principle of humanity, which I think is the same thing.

But I want to reference something said by Bishop DiMarzio, who gave the Mass in Brooklyn on that Sunday. He said, "Those who will risk their lives to save someone they don't know—they embody the hessence of what it means to be Christian." You could replace that word "Christian" with "human," and you could replace that word "Christian" with "American." In recognition of that principle, the Mass was given in honor of a whole crew of Brooklyn firefighters who lost their lives, and we had the great honor to be incorporated in that Mass, performing Mozart's *Requiem*.

That same principle was honored at the "Tunnel to Towers" event, to which a few organizers went exactly one week ago last Sunday. This is an annual event of the Stephen Siller Tunnel to Towers Foundation, which draws people nationwide. Twenty-five thousand registered for it.

This is an event in honor of Stephen Siller. It is a run and walk, recreating the steps of this fallen firefighter, who was off duty at the time the towers were hit. Seeing that the towers had been hit, he got in his truck, got to the Brooklyn Tunnel, and couldn't get through. So he got out the truck, put on 60 pounds of equipment, and ran to the Towers. He saved an unknown number lives before losing his own. This is an event that draws *thousands* of Americans. Obviously we talked to first responders, we talked to people who lost their loved ones, we talked to Americans who didn't lose anybody. So, this is something which is American. It is a principle that is human, it's Christian, it's American. And it was a principle that you could say was an arc from the concerts to this victory in JASTA, which I would describe as nothing less than a miracle, what you just said.

LaRouche: Let me try to clarify a ghost, a ghost which happened when the two towers collapsed. It went out from Boston airport. The Saudi perpetrators grabbed the citizens in two concentrations in Boston, and each of these planes went into the towers with the passengers. This happened.

It was done by the Saudis themselves. It was done with the consent of the friends of the Saudis. I was a witness from a different tower, and I gave a record of this. I observed, with my own eyes, what happened on that day. That whole record has been there *since that time*.

Only recently, in the most recent days, we have finally escaped that horrible experience. And we should take pleasure in the fact that we have *finally* pulled ourselves together, and we have also *thrown the Saudis out of the United States*! [applause]

Restore the Souls, Build the Minds

Question: Hi, Lyn! Alvin here. It's really good to see you. I want to go back to what I raised last week with Dave Christie. I wasn't very satisfied with what I presented to him.

What I was trying to express,— and it even grows more, because you referenced it earlier in the week, when you talked about how one should expect the Devil to react when you do him harm. I was talking to Dave about

> **LaRouche,** 1995: "When you can communicate something, not by words, but by paradox, that paradox now becomes an object of consciousness, of thought, an intellectual object which has no sense perception, no sound, no visual image; it exists independent of all senses, and yet it is a definite object. You can show that this object increases man's power over nature, and that in no other way can man's power over nature be increased."

this. I characterized it as Obama being Hitler in the bunker. But what I really meant to say was that he has a Nero personality, and what appears to be, with the people surrounding him now, a type of flight forward.

Now, you always say, "This is a bluff, this is a bluff," but what I'm raising to you is that when you actually think about this, when you actually work on it, and you start talking about it, I was really just thinking about it: It's really very unnerving. I also remember, years ago, your saying there are a lot of bad people, but there are really very, very few *evil* people, and then even less that can even face evil. And it seems like these things are heating up to such a point so, I guess if it's a question to you, how do we keep our nerve and hold steady, without,— I don't want to enjoy victories too much. We have to stay alert and keep moving, but how? Talk to us about that.

LaRouche: Very simple. We have to rebuild the United States, and more than the United States—we have to build the world. And that's it. That's our mission. And it means not just the infrastructure and so forth, but it means the souls and the minds of the people. And to build up a population which is rejuvenated and capable of carrying out great victories.

To Grasp What Mankind *Must Become*

Phil Rubinstein: Yes, hi Lyn.

I want to pick up on the question of creating a new science, or recreating science. We've come out of the 20th Century, this destruction of the science, which I think is in particular a destruction of the idea of the human mind. You mentioned yesterday the idea of teasing young people into thinking about science and discovery, and, of course—in the case that you're always talking about, the connection to great art and great compositio—to tease them into thinking about how to create a new science, or creating science anew. And I think, even in my own case, certainly the great problem of Einstein versus Bohr, which I think was a question of whether the human mind doesn't really have the right to assess the universe, or whether it can merely say things about observations.

And then I think you're calling on us to have some kind of discussion like that or beyond that, and I'd like to ask you on the four principles—to follow through with the victory on JASTA—do we have to do that from the standpoint of creating science itself, addressing questions that we barely even know right now? Will we have a whole new Solar system? We have access to galaxies. Is that going to be essential, or how we should make it essential to implementing the whole package?

LaRouche: We have to build up fast, *very fast*, the greatest growth of productivity inside nations, now. And that's what we have to do. In other words, we have to understand what mankind *is* and what mankind *must be* and must *become*, *fast*. We can do that, but we have to catch the idea, and we have not yet caught the idea. But we can. So, why don't you start doing it?

Think Beyond Glass-Steagall

Question: Good afternoon, Mr. LaRouche, this is J—. Glad to see you. I just come away from Brooklyn. I have here a pamphlet that I found in my little archive space in my house, that says, "Tantamount to Treason." I'm sure you remember this one. OK.

Glass-Steagall. Let's talk about Glass-Steagall. I became known as the "Glass-Steagall lady" in my union, and I think that now that we've had this victory with JASTA, the networks that we have created, the people we've talked to, to get the JASTA bill veto over-ridden, can be mobilized for Glass-Steagall added to our mobilization that we've always had for Glass-Steagall. And as you were just saying, even go beyond the localized mobilization to people of other nations; we can also talk about what Glass-Steagall is and why it is absolutely necessary that we pass Glass-Steagall. And *that* will get rid of Obama, also.

So, as I see it, and I want you to comment on it, please, that mobilization is right now, and I'm really,

Ludwig van Beethoven wrote, "There is much to be done on earth; do it soon!" and spoke of his art "as a means of relieving needy humanity." In 1823, he wrote to his student, the Archduke Rudolf, "There is nothing higher than to approach the Godhead more nearly than other mortals, and by means of that contact to spread the rays of the Godhead through the human race."

really happy about the victory, phone calls that were made, and all the things that were done, and now we move to tantamount to treason, the Glass-Steagall Act has to be reinstated.

LaRouche: Well, the answer is to your question, is when are we going to get started and get going on what we have to do? Because we have undone things before us. We talk about it, we look at it. We haven't done it. What we have to do is get the people together, in the proper sense, and get out there and do the work, actually make it resonate, an actual Renaissance of, shall we say, Manhattan. Start with Manhattan. Let's have a renaissance, a true renaissance in Manhattan. And then do the same kind of thing in other areas. You've got to get the juices going inside the relevant people so that they are actually cranked up, ready to do the job.

Question: Hi, it's C— again. I noticed that, when it comes to the United States, our country, whenever there is a country in peril, or they have some kind of political issue going on, we always come in to try to help them and intervene. And I know that in order to save someone's life you must be able to save yourself in order to save others, but how come we're doing that, knowing full well that we have other problems we need to take care of first? That's my question.

LaRouche: We have a problem, and the big prob-

Abraham Heschel, the Orthodox rabbi who marched with Martin Luther King, wrote in 1973:

"The soul is 'a part of God from above,' but man thinks he is all from below, all made of dust. Every man must think of himself as a stairway set on the ground, its top reaching heaven. It is within his power to affect what should happen in the upper worlds. The greatest sin of man is to forget that he is a prince—that he has royal power. All worlds are in need of exaltation, and everyone is charged to lift what is low, to unite what lies apart, to advance what is left behind. It is as if all worlds, above and below, are full of expectancy, of sacred goals to be reached ..."

Wikipedia

lem is called education, public education. It includes universities; it includes other institutions of that type. What you have to do, first of all, is get busy in cleaning up education, by educating people *seriously*, not just "at it."

Impeach Obama, Send Brennan to Prison

Burke: Hi, Lyn. I've been asked to give a little report. So hopefully you'll get a kick out of this, and maybe it will be worth ending with.

On Monday night, two nights before the Wednesday veto override vote in the Congress, John Brennan came to the scene of the crime. He came to the 9/11 Memorial, the museum that's right there at Ground Zero in Lower Manhattan. There was an audience of about 200 people who, as far as I could gather, were mainly reporters, and FBI and CIA agents. [Lyn laughs] I don't know who else would want to hear him speak, other than people who have to, for their jobs.

But we went and we knew that we had to present something that would give people some courage leading into the vote on Wednesday. So the four of us, Ian who's sitting right next to me, and my wife, and Maria, who was up here earlier, we went in and we sat down. And we had a plan that we were just going to tell the

truth, and actually there was a moment where we were wondering if it was going to be a moment of silence. And one of us said, if that happens, then what the 9/11 victims will have wanted is for us to interrupt that moment of silence to tell the truth, and that would really be what they would want people to hear.

So as soon as Mr. Brennan came out and began his apologia for the Saudis, we stood up, one after another, over the space of about a half hour or 45 minutes, and we looked him right in the eyes. We stood up, we pointed at him, and said, "You are a traitor on behalf of the Saudis who ran the 9/11 operation, killing thousands. Obama should be impeached. The JASTA bill must pass. And you should go to jail." And one after another, we were carried out by the police. So that's what happened. That's my report. [applause]

LaRouche: It can happen. It could happen on a larger or smaller scale, as the case may be.

Question: Lyn, this is my second time, having the opportunity of saying hello to you, and again I salute you. At Carnegie Hall on October 6, 7, and 8, the Simon Bolivar Symphony Orchestra from Venezuela will be performing. I have details on that, if people want to ask me or contact Carnegie Hall. Thank you.

LaRouche: I want to suggest a correction about the fraud being delivered in Brazil. The threat to Dilma Rousseff in Brazil is a tragedy. It's a threat. And there are other threats which are coming on in these areas, and we have to concentrate specifically on these kinds of problems. If you don't do it, you find you will undermine your own ability to think, and to act.

Cornyn's Attack on the Monarchy

Renee Sigerson: On this question of public education: Senator Cornyn, when he delivered this unexpected summary, said at the end that there were two ways that the Obama administration was confusing people on the question of JASTA, but they were related. Number one, was by implying that somehow we would injure our "sovereign immunity" if we address this, and he said this was the most ridiculous thing, because he said this is a matter that's been under discussion for decades, and there's nothing new about Congress clarifying this concept.

But then he added something which was really quite unusual. He said, "Let me also tell Americans, sovereign immunity is a concept which does *not* derive from American law. To let you know, it is a reference in our Anglo-American roots," and he used that expression, "Anglo-American roots," to reference the King, and he just left it hanging. And everybody in political positions in the United States knows that it's *this* political movement which been howling unceasingly about the repulsive British monarchical influence and oligarchical influence in the United States, and in a certain sense, he opened the curtain to saying, "Look, we're going to have to look at this."

And when you talk about public education, John brought it up in the class last night, that when you were twelve years old, you listed all of the leading philosophers of Western civilization, and it was the obvious British ones, and then it was Leibniz and Kant also; but you went on to decide who was your favorite, and Leibniz won the contest.

But the reality of the situation is that British philosophical liberalism is pervasive in the entire society that we live in, and I think part of the challenge of this revolutionary mindset that you are indicating that we have to move towards, is that we really have to get people to give up the idea that we are simply creatures that simply "seek pleasure and try to avoid pain," which is what the entire British philosophical belief amounts to. There really is no other content! That we're here to seek pleasure and avoid pain!

We must convey that that is *not* the meaning of our lives, and we must liberate people from this silly, pedestrian, idiotic mindset. We must make available to people—because we have it permeate everything that *we're* doing—what the deeper meaning of this finite, precious human existence is. That's what we really need to celebrate, and that's what we shared in this experience with the people who died. That was the whole point: That they did not die in vain, but they force us to restore our commitment to this sacred concept.

So I think there really was something deeper that happened that day, that we must carry with us, even though this one particular example is one that I caught on to, I'm sure other things happened that were of that kind, in that staged presentation on the floor of the Senate.

LaRouche: It's relevant, it's quite relevant. But I think we should have a much more elaborated explanation of what that means. I think we should do that.

Speed: We're at the close now, Lyn. I thought I heard a task get assigned to the Manhattan Project. I heard Glass-Steagall, I heard create a Renaissance in Manhattan, I heard that Wall Street has lost the war. Ideas come up and you can tell when we're not thinking. Correct me if I'm wrong, this is what we're supposed to do next, right?

LaRouche: Why not?

Speed: OK, just wanted to make sure I was clear. Would you like to say anything else?

LaRouche: I think we ought to expand our functioning and spread our activity a little more. We're not getting enough action.

Speed: Yep! OK. Well, I think everybody understands what that means—I hope!

LaRouche: They do!

Speed: We'll be seeing you next week, we devoutly hope!

LaRouche: OK, have fun! [applause]

HELGA ZEPP-LAROUCHE

Bringing America Into the New Paradigm

This is an edited transcription of the keynote remarks of Helga Zepp-LaRouche to the Houston Seminar, Saturday, Oct. 1. She was introduced by Kesha Rogers.

Kesha Rogers: Good morning everyone, I'm very happy to see our audience here this morning in Houston for this very special event and occasion that we're going to be having here today for our day-long seminar, called "A Symposium To Prepare You for Victory." This is titled, "Unleashing the Creative Nature of Man."

We have a special guest with us today, the founder and chairwoman of the Schiller Institute, Mrs. Helga Zepp-LaRouche, who will be addressing us this morning. And I think Helga's address is coming at a very timely point for mankind and for the nation in history. And I'd like to say good evening to Helga, who's addressing us now from Europe. And I want to go ahead and let Helga get started with her remarks and then what I'm going to do is come back up and fill you in on the the treats we have for you over the course of the day.

We will be making presentations regarding this unleashing of the human creative identity and the Renaissance culture, the new paradigm for mankind that we are now in the midst of and seeking to create.

And Helga will start us off with that discussion. After Helga's remarks, we will open it up for questions and answers, and then after that we will continue with

Helga Zepp-LaRouche

EIRNS

our program for the day. So, again, thank you Helga for joining, and thank you all for being here this morning. [applause]

Helga Zepp-LaRouche: Anybody who watches the very rapidly changing strategic situation—which almost creates a new unbelievable moment every day—is probably wondering what direction this will take. We have on the one side, a very, very dangerous confrontation exploding from the side of the United States and NATO against Russia. When the ceasefire negotiations between Secretary of State John Kerry and Foreign Minister Sergei Lavrov of Russia broke down, basically because there are certain forces within the United States who did not want it to succeed, that put us back on a potential confrontation between the West, and especially the United States, and Russia.

This is a situation which comes from a certain paradigm of thinking. It is a result of the fact that the United States insists that it is the United States which sets the rules around the world and keeps a unipolar world, which is no longer really in existence.

Underlying all of this, you have the immediate danger of a blowout of the financial system. The most obvious case right now is Deutsche Bank. Deutsche Bank is the largest so-called German bank—it's not really German any more because it's living in London and in Wall Street—but it has a derivatives exposure of

DoD photo by Air Force Tech. Sgt. Brigitte N. Brantley

Defense Secretary Ash Carter addresses sailors aboard the USS Carl Vinson in San Diego, Sept. 29, 2016. Carter is on a trip to discuss the U.S. "mission" in the Asia-Pacific region.

$42 trillion, and every large bank in the world is a counter-party, and those banks are also loaded down with derivatives.

Deutsche Bank could go under. Its stock has dropped like a stone in the last year—on Friday, at one point its stock even dipped below 10 euros. At that point, people were really panicking. All the financial media were saying that this is the potential new 2008, this is the "Lehman Brothers moment of Deutsche Bank." The financial media started to show no respect for Angela Merkel, the Chancellor of Germany, by saying she bungled that crisis again, because she had said a couple of days ago that, "If there is a new crisis of Deutsche Bank, the German government is not going to bail it out," and that led to a complete speculative attack which made everything worse. One financial analyst was reported in Bloomberg News today, saying that these "zombie banks" soon will create a "zombie economy."

At this point, you have the coincidence of these two crises: A strategic showdown, where Ash Carter was travelling to U.S. military bases in the last week. In North Dakota at an Air Force base, inspecting the B-52 bomber which is nuclear capable, he said, "The Russians have mentioned the possibility of using nuclear weapons, but even if there would be a conventional attack the use of nuclear weapons is not unthinkable. It has not been used since 1945, but one should not rely on the fact that it remains like that.

Obviously, if you take these two dynamics: (1) the new Cold War which is already very, very close to turning into a hot war in Syria, which in turn could lead to a global showdown between the West, and Russia, and China, because Russia and China now have an extremely close strategic alliance, and (2) the financial meltdown, which is much, much worse than 2008, because all the central banks have used up their so-called "tools," quantitative easing, and negative interest rates. They're talking about "helicopter money" and that is about as bad as it gets, so, is there any hope that civilization can pull itself out of this?

The Way Out

I think there is. And for all those people who normally say, "oh, you can't do anything anyway, because those powers up there, they're too powerful," I think a recent development really has proven these people to be utterly wrong. When a couple of days ago, both houses of Congress, the Senate and the House of Representatives, voted to override Obama's veto in respect to the JASTA bill, this came as a big surprise, to everybody, I guess, including ourselves.

There was a 15-year-long battle, where the families of the victims of Sept. 11, had courageously fought to get the 28 pages released, and they were putting pressure on the U.S. government to have the right to sue Saudi Arabia for their possible involvement in 9/11—which, after the publication of the 28 pages, was pretty obvious.

But then, in the last four weeks, something additional happened, that has certainly been completely overlooked by Obama for sure. It has certainly also been overlooked by the Saudis, and it has caught even the Congress and the Senate by surprise.

We organized four concerts of Mozart's *Requiem* and African-American Spirituals, which commemorated the fifteenth anniversary of the 9/11 attacks, with an attendance of about 4,000 people who watched in person and listened to these performances, in addition to many more via live audio-visual transmission and on the Internet afterwards. It was evident if you watched it, that everybody who participated in these concerts was completely transformed. People were moved in the deepest part of their souls, in their hearts. Many of the family members and firemen and police officers who participated in these concerts, said that even though they had commemorated this terrible catastrophe every year for 15 years, never had anything like what they had experienced with Mozart's *Requiem*, happened to them.

It is extremely important that we understand what has happened with these concerts. Because, for those of you who know Friedrich Schiller and especially one of his later plays, called *The Bride of Messina*, he has a beautiful introduction with the title "On the Role of Chorus." And there he describes, and he doesn't mean the

EIRNS/Stuart Lewis

Schiller Institute chorus performing Mozart's Requiem at the Co-Cathedral of St. Joseph, Brooklyn, NY, as part of a four-concert living memorial by the Schiller Institute, on the weekend of 9/11/2016, to victims of the 9/11/2001 attacks.

musical chorus, he means the ancient Greek chorus which was always part of the ancient Classical dramas. He says there: The power of great art is that it creates a force in people which does not end when the performance—when the great piece of music or drama ends, but it creates a lasting power in the person who participates in such an experience. The reason is, he says, is that great Classical art is not looking to set man free temporarily, but to set him free truly, and therefore this power is increased in man when he participates in that.

And it was precisely those concerts which gave the additional, I would say, inspiration, spark of absolute sovereignty and absolute sublime power of will and courage which the family members could then transmit to even those hardened Congressmen and Senators. I watched the Congressional debate live and I must say, some of these Senators did say things which were quite surprising. And that power, of the fight for justice inspired by Classical music, was proven to be more powerful than all the millions of dollars of Saudi Arabia and their disgusting law firms and public relations firms which they had hired to put pressure on the Congress to not override Obama's veto.

This is extremely important, because Mr. LaRouche yesterday said that we have to add that quality into the fight, because if you stay on the level of pragmatic policy, the fight cannot be won on that level. And what Mr. LaRouche also stated, is that we have to add a com-

pletely new desire to find new scientific discoveries—to really go for scientific breakthroughs in the knowledge of what is the true identity of man. Why is the human species in existence? What is our role in the Solar system? What is the role of mankind in the Galaxy?

This demand that we have to go for a completely new definition of what science is, is very interesting. Science is neither some mathematical formula, nor some pragmatic gimmick, but is a fundamental understanding about the role of the human mind in the Universe, showing precisely the direction in which the next scientific breakthroughs have to occur. That is precisely what Nicholas of Cusa had already said in the 15th Century, that every newly born human being recapitulates the entire history of the universe, practically in his own mind, by learning the knowledge of mankind up to the level of the knowledge of his time. Then, based on that knowledge, he can define the next step necessary for a breakthrough.

This understanding of the development of new science challenges the way people think that science has progressed. Scientific progress is not some kind of an awkward discovery somebody makes in their garage and then gets a patent for this discovery, and somehow that's how scientific progress occurs. No. Cusa, and in that same light, Lyndon LaRouche says, man can with absolute certainty determine where mankind must go if mankind is to continue to exist.

The Necessary New Paradigm

What are these next steps? We need a new paradigm and that new paradigm obviously, in light of what I said in the beginning about the two strategic crises which are now facing the existence of civilization, must overcome geopolitics and also overcome the idea that a nation has a legitimate right to pursue its own national interests.

What has to occur instead is that we have to proceed from the ideal of the one, unified mankind which informs our decisions first, and then the national interest comes after that.

That new paradigm requires a shift in thinking. It is a paradigm which is so fundamentally different from the paradigm which now governs the world, including the world of geopolitics, that the shift must be as big or bigger than the paradigm shift which separated the Middle Ages from modern times.

Cardinal Nicholas of Cusa, 1401-1464.

For those who have read about the Middle Ages, this was like the 14th Century for example, a period which was absolutely horrible. You had Black Death, you had witchcraft, you had people going crazy over the Black Death, you have universities dominated by Scholasticism, by Aristotelianism, the new Peripatetics, and this was a method which was a complete dead-end of thinking. No new knowledge could come from this kind of geometry.

The learning of that era was similar, in a certain sense, to the kind of stuff which is being taught in our universities today, which is based on mathematics, on health economics—which is really a way of defining triage in the health sector, deductionist thinking, reductionist processes, and produces no new knowledge. No new qualitative knowledge can be produced by that method of thinking.

Cusa Rejected Axioms

So what was the beginning, the most important step in the new paradigm of the modern times? It was actually the thinking of such people as especially Nicholas of Cusa. He very consciously rejected all the axioms that went along with the Middle Ages and Scholasticism and Aristotle. And he said, I'm thinking something which never has been thought by any human being before. He developed a method of thinking which he called the "coincidence of opposites," which was the idea that the One has a higher power and a higher magnitude than the Many.

Nicholas of Cusa, who was a Cardinal in the 15th Century, developed this idea through a theological argument by saying that the One is God and that the Many, being the universe and all created things, are unfolded out of this One. And therefore you have to be able to think like a second god, you never will be like God, but you have to apply the *vis creativa* of God, the creative power of God, and then you become a second god.

Now, in his *Docta Ignorantia* he developed these ideas in the most powerful way and if you haven't read it yet, please go home and read this absolutely groundbreaking work, which was immediately attacked by the same Scholastic professors in the universities and the clergy, who felt completely threatened, and they accused Nicholas of Cusa of being a pantheist, because if Cusa says God is in everything, and everything is in God, then that's pantheism, which, of course, it is not. Joseph Wenck was one of those who vociferously attacked Cusa, and after some years Cusa chose to counter his criticisms.

Cusa said: Obviously, this poor Mr. Wenck has not understood what I'm talking about, that it is a completely different way of thinking; that if you are on the level of Aristotle, you are just seeing contradictions and you don't see the higher level of reason. He said: My thinking, the thinking on the level of the coincidence of opposites, is like—and he used a very nice pedagogical way to describe it—he said, it's like standing on a high tower, and you're looking down, and what you see when you're looking down is, you see the hunter, you see the hunted, and the process of hunting. While the Aristotelian is either the hunter or the hunted, but he never sees the process.

He then appeals to people to elevate their thinking and make the mental jump over what he calls the "wall of the *coincidentia oppositorum*" which is a kind of intuitive thinking. It is basically that kind of thinking which we need to accomplish and what goes along with that, is the ability to think a completely new level of relations among men, among nations, to proceed from humanity as a whole.

And one country which has now already proposed very concretely making that jump, based on that level of thinking, is China: It proposed a new level of relations among nations, based on the respect for complete sovereignty of the other, respect for the different social system of the other country, of non-interference, and basically that is the opposite of what Obama said recently in an article in the *Washington Post*, where he said "the United States sets the rules, and not China."

Xinhua

China continues to expand high-speed rail construction, to eventually link 80% of China's cities with high-speed rail. Here, four CRH380D high-speed trains, which have a maximum speed of 380 km/hr.

Positive U.S. Role Is Available

For the United States this would mean going back to the outlook of John Quincy Adams, who in his foreign policy had established exactly the same idea, that the United States was a republic and that it should have a perfect alliance of sovereign republics, with non-interference and respect for their respective sovereignty.

Obviously, our economic proposal, that the New Silk Road must become the World Land-Bridge, is based exactly on that type of thinking. Then you can work together on international projects for the development of every part of the world, but you do it with the full respect for sovereignty of the other, instead of trying to dominate the systems of economics and finance.

It would mean, for example, that the United States would cooperate in such a "win-win" perspective. Now, what would that mean? Would it mean the United States would have a Silk Road? The United States, which is now falling apart in terms of infrastructure, would have a system of fast trains, like China does. By 2020, China wants to have every major city connected to a fast train system which would travel at 450 kph. For the United States this would mean the immediate construction of 50-100,000 miles of fast train systems connecting all the major cities, creating some new cities, including science cities, and simply participating in a completely different economic system, as Franklin D. Roosevelt

did with the New Deal, but this time geared towards the 21st Century.

Global Glass-Steagall

It would also mean immediately addressing the bankrupt financial system, by installing a new financial architecture in the tradition of Roosevelt, which would have a global Glass-Steagall system, which may be forced upon the world more quickly than anyone may think: because if Deutsche Bank goes bankrupt, the whole financial system comes down. Mr. LaRouche and myself proposed a [couple of weeks ago], to go back to the model of Deutsche Bank as it was before Alfred Herrhausen was assassinated in 1989. This would mean putting Deutsche Bank under a bankruptcy/insolvency commission, to unwind in an orderly fashion the very complex derivatives, which are very interwoven with all the major banks internationally. Most of these derivatives cannot be paid, therefore you have to write them down.

And then you have to protect the business model in Deutsche Bank, the part which is engaged in commercial banking and enlarge that aspect of the bank by making that the only business plan of Deutsche Bank. This would mean applying a sort of local Glass-Steagall to Deutsche Bank. Given the size of Deutsche Bank, such a move would immediately make necessary

A railway construction project in Pakistan, along the route of the China-Pakistan Economic Corridor, carried out with Chinese funding and cooperation.

a global Glass-Steagall, because the derivatives exposure is so intertwined with all the other banks, that it simply would be the only alternative to a complete breakdown into chaos.

It would also mean cooperating on the basis of such a global Glass-Steagall system with national banking systems of each of these sovereign countries. Now when we're talking about the World Land-Bridge, we're talking about projects which last, in terms of realization, 20, 30, 40 years, 50 years. However, with the speed of construction that the Chinese have demonstrated in the recent period, it would probably not require 50 years, but probably 25. But it still would require national banks in each participating country. It would require compensating for the fact that some of the countries are large, like Russia, with 11 time zones, have very few people, large supplies of raw materials. Some countries are very small and landlocked like Slovakia, while others are very, very poor, like Eritrea. There are many, many differences, and you need to set up a new credit system which takes these differences into account, because the new credits given by these national banks cannot be paid back before the investment realizes what they were meant for, i.e. producing the necessary productivity increase of the labor force and the industries of the countries participating. So you need clearing houses which take care of these differences and long-term and short-term commitments.

That is then the new credit system, which would be a sort of New Bretton Woods system which would go along with the World Land-Bridge. China has already called for that, with the demand for a new financial architecture, and has created a parallel banking system with the AIIB, the New Development Bank, the Silk Road Fund, the Maritime Silk Road Fund, and the Shanghai Cooperation Bank. So the alternative system is already in place, and if the trans-Atlantic sector, Europe, and the United States, would get rid of their casino economies, they could immediately be integrated into this already-existing financial system. So it is absolutely possible and within reach.

China's World Development Offer

Xi Jinping not only demanded that the world economy, following the G-20 meeting in Hangzhou in the beginning of September, must be based on innovation. "Innovation" is not just, as I said, some arbitrary innovation, but it must address the fundamental requirements of the world economy. This means, in the physical economy terms of Lyndon LaRouche, that the increase of the energy-flux density must provide the basis for the increase in the relative potential population density of the planet, and that must be the scientific yardstick of whether an innovation is actually productive or not. A lot of the innovation which takes place now is in areas which are not productive at all, and the new innovation must be geared towards increasing the real processes in the Universe.

It is highly interesting that Xi Jinping demanded that Chinese scientists make fundamental breakthroughs in four areas:

• The evolution of the Universe

• What are the laws of the development of the Universe?

• Third, the laws of the human mind

• Fourth, the laws of life, what is life? How does it originate, how does it occur?

And these are all touching upon the kind of fundamental questions, what Lyndon LaRouche called for yesterday, and obviously, this is the direction in which we have to go.

You have heard a lot from Kesha and others about the absolutely fantastic world outlook of Krafft Ehricke, who called for the extraterrestrial imperative, as the necessary next phase of the development of mankind.

Krafft Ehricke was a close friend of ours, and especially in the last years of his life, I had many conversations with him about the relationship between science and culture. And he was absolutely convinced that the efforts of the Schiller Institute were absolutely crucial, because, he said, we have to add the aesthetical education of man to scientific progress, since technology is never good or bad. It is man which brings it to a good or an evil use. Therefore, he said, the crucial question is that we ennoble the human species, which is exactly the question of the aesthetical education.

This is why we put such a big emphasis on beauty, and that art must be beautiful, because only then does it accomplish this ennobling of the human soul. Beauty, Schiller says, is very important because it is both a quality of the senses, because the senses are perceptive of beauty, but it is also in the realm of reason, because what is beauty is not a question of experience, but it is a question of the definition of the mind, of reason.

Therefore, Schiller says, we have to educate the emotions, which are related to the senses, but not identical with the senses. We have to educate these emotions up to the level of reason, so that man can blindly follow what the emotions are saying, without ever losing control or going to a lower level.

So therefore, he said, we have to educate every human being to become a beautiful soul, so that people can blindly follow their instincts because their instincts would never tell them anything which is not guided by reason, and therefore, freedom and necessity, passion and duty, must become the same.

I think that that is an emotional development which is the only way that man will master the requirements of the extraterrestrial imperative, because if man does not become more noble and better, I don't think we are going to make it.

Therefore, Schiller added to the question of beauty, the question of the Sublime, the Sublime being that quality which in a certain sense makes man great even if he is confronted with tragedy and catastrophe, because he has bound his identity to a higher cause and higher principles than those which can threaten his mortal life. And I think it is that Sublime quality which is evoked by great Classical art and what we have seen by the power unleashed in the concerts leading to the absolute breakthrough in the fight in the Congress.

This kind of thinking is necessary to make the kinds of breakthroughs Lyn is demanding. Nicholas of Cusa said the only people who are capable of making these kinds of necessary breakthroughs are people who are thinking on the level of the *coincidentia oppositorum*, the coincidence of opposites, because only if you are thinking on that level, do you have something which Lyndon LaRouche called "prescience." Nicholas says, the person who makes a discovery has to know already ahead of time what he is looking for, because if you just discover something and do not know what you were looking for, you do not even know if what you have found is the right thing.

Therefore, it is that kind of creative intuition, which is what is really at stake, and that quality happens to be the same emotional mental quality that you need to write Classical poetry, to write classical drama, to make a scientific discovery, it all comes from the same faculty of your mind. And we have to educate the entire population, so that they reject the present pragmatic or even Satanic joy in the here and now, the lust for the senses, or just degraded kind of entertainment, and we have to get people to taste the sweetness of the thinking of a creative person, because that is the only way in which mankind will become truly human.

And I have a beautiful idea of what the new paradigm can be: Just imagine if we get the best minds of each culture in each nation, relating to each other in love and admiration for the creative powers of the other one, like the great space scientists who are working together, or the astronauts who all report what the viewpoint is when you look at our planet from space. The idea that people will relate to each other like the relationship between Einstein and Max Planck, or among Schiller, Humboldt, Körner, in other words, or the Humboldt brothers. In a certain sense, we have to fight for that kind of humanity, where people respect and love each other for their creative powers, and have no greater passion than to further the creative abilities of their contemporary citizens and fellow human beings.

And I think we are on the verge of that. I think that with the recent victory, the power for the good has been demonstrated, and I think we have to absolutely carry that forward: And then victory is within reach. [applause]

Every Day Counts In Today's Showdown To Save Civilization

That's why you need EIR's **Daily Alert Service**, a strategic overview compiled with the input of Lyndon LaRouche, and delivered to your email 5 days a week.

For example: On Jan. 7, EIR's Daily Alert featured the British hand behind the pattern of global provocations toward war. Of special note is British Intelligence's role in instigating the Saudi Kingdom's attempt to set off a Sunni-Shia war. This religious war has been the intent of British strategy since the Blair-Bush attack on Iraq in 2003.

We also uniquely update you regularly on the progress toward the release of the suppressed 28 pages of the Congressional Inquiry on 9/11, which would expose the Saudi role.

Every edition highlights the reality of the impending financial crash/bail-in policies that would realize the British goal of mass depopulation.

This is intelligence you need to act on, if we are going to survive as a nation and a species. Can you really afford to be without it?

THURSDAY, JANUARY 7, 2016

Volume 2, Number 97

EIR Daily Alert Service

P. O. Box 17390, WASHINGTON, DC 20041-0390

- British Crown Pushing War and Genocide in 2016
- Financial Mudslide Goes On; Monetarist Tyranny Gloats over Bail-Ins
- Moody's Downgrades Portugal's Novo Banco
- Puerto Rico's Default: It's Every Vulture for Himself
- Wide Glass-Steagall Debate Set Off Again by Sanders Speech
- MI6 Mouthpiece Evans-Pritchard Touts Persian Gulf Chaos
- North Korea Tests a Miniaturized Hydrogen Bomb
- Uighur Terrorists Found in Indonesia
- Foreign Investors Are Flocking In to China

EDITORIAL

British Crown Pushing War and Genocide in 2016

Survival and 'Justice for the Future' Demand Obama's Removal Now!

by Robert Ingraham

Section 4 of the 25th Amendment to the U.S. Constitution reads:

> Whenever the Vice President and a majority of either the principal officers of the executive departments or of such other body as Congress may by law provide, transmit to the President pro tempore of the Senate and the Speaker of the House of Representatives their written declaration that the President is unable to discharge the powers and duties of his office, the Vice President shall immediately assume the powers and duties of the office as Acting President.

According to the precise wording of this amendment, action may be initiated by the Vice President, members of the Cabinet, or *such other body as Congress may by law provide* to remove the President of the United States if any of these individuals or elected officials are of the view that the sitting President is *unable to discharge the powers and duties of his office*. There is no requirement for illness or physical disability. There is no requirement for any specific list of reasons for taking such action. There is no requirement for extended hearings, testimony, or other bureaucratic procedures. Given a clear necessity for the President's removal and a recognition that he is unable to discharge his duties—in accordance with his Oath of Office—action may be taken immediately—*action may be taken today*—to remove him.

In the Wake of the JASTA Vote

This issue of the *Executive Intelligence Review* contains an accompanying article "Congress Delivers a Deafening Blow to Obama and the Anglo-Saudis" by Jeffrey Steinberg. That article clearly defines the treachery and treason of Barack Obama in regard to the protection he has personally provided to the government of Saudi Arabia as to their role in the 9/11 attacks which

LPAC

LaRouche PAC organizers in Manhattan.

killed 3,000 American citizens. At the same time, that same article describes the courage of certain individual members of Congress—and other Americans—in fighting for justice for the 9/11 families and survivors, justice, in fact, for all Americans in finally bringing their government to act morally and constitutionally.

This was not merely a victory on a simple piece of legislation; it was potentially a transformative victory, one which holds the promise for those involved in the JASTA fight, and others still to be recruited to this effort, to effect a profound change in morality and personal responsibility within Congress and the American populace. As Jeff Steinberg puts it in his article, "Champions are needed."

What must be understood at this moment are two

DoD/Glenn Fawcett

DoD/Air Force Tech. Sgt. Brigitte N. Brantley

The Obama Administration has unleashed a torrent of verbal and diplomatic attacks on Russia. Former Pentagon press secretary and current State Department spokesman Adm. John Kirby, left, and Secretary of Defense Ash Carter in front of a B52 strategic bomber at Minot Air Force Base, N.D.

interrelated lessons: first, that we are not fighting for single-issue successes; second, that the past crimes of Barack Obama are not the primary reason for the urgency of his removal from office. It is the danger, the paramount imminent danger, of allowing Obama to remain in office for the next three months which must be faced.

Syria, Russia and China

During this past week, as the armed forces of the Syrian Government have met with growing success in their fight to liberate the city of Aleppo from terrorist control, spokesmen for the Obama Administration have unleashed a torrent of verbal and diplomatic attacks on Russia. Those words have been accompanied with actions. On three separate occasions—at the Minot Air Force Base in North Dakota, at the Kirtland Air Force Base in New Mexico, and aboard the aircraft carrier USS Carl Vinson at San Diego—U.S. Defense Secretary Ash Carter delivered speeches threatening Russia with nuclear attack. In the Kirtland AFB speech, Carter was explicit that the Obama Administration—without any Congressional consultation or approval—reserves the right to carry out a "first strike" thermo-nuclear attack on Russia, and in San Diego Carter listed "Russian aggression," not terrorism, as the primary threat to U.S. national security. One day after his San Diego speech, Carter traveled to Hawaii where, in public remarks, he

delivered similar provocative accusations against China.

While all of this was occurring, the United States, France, and Britain convened an emergency session of the U.N. Security Council on Sept. 25 to try to block Syria's successful military offensive in Aleppo. At that meeting, the American Ambassador to the United Nations—and longtime Obama intimate—Samantha Power, accused Russia of "barbarism" for supporting Syria in the fight against terrorism. Incredibly, Power also accused Russia of bombing "first responders," the very category of people whom Obama dishonored in his veto of the JASTA legislation.

On Sept. 28 Obama State Department spokesman Admiral John Kirby publicly stated that if Russia continues in its support for the legitimate Syrian government, it will face the consequences of "attacks against Russian interests, perhaps even Russian cities, and Russia will continue to send troops home in body bags, and they will continue to lose resources—even, perhaps, more aircraft." In response, Russian Defense Ministry spokesman Major General Igor Konashenkov said, "Even the slightest hints of a threat to our soldiers and Russian citizens must be excluded from this dialogue. The matter of safety of Russian citizens, wherever they may be, is not up for bargaining. It is our main and unconditional priority."

On Sept. 29 two former high-ranking officials of the Obama Administration, Derek Chollet and Frederic

Derek Chollet twitter page   cc.www.stephan-roehl.de

Two former high-ranking members of the Obama Administration, Derek Chollet, left, and Frederic Hof, right, are calling for a no-fly zone to be imposed over Syria.

Hof, published twin editorials in the *Washington Post*, in what amounts to as an open call for total war against Russia. Both call for direct U.S. military action against President Assad's military forces—a direct violation of both International Law and the U.S. Constitution—and Chollet demands the immediate implementation of a U.S.-imposed "no-fly" zone over Syria, an action which will absolutely result in direct clashes between U.S. and Russian military forces. In an interview given by Virginia State Senator and Syria expert Richard Black to LaRouche PAC on Sept. 28, Black warns that any attempt by the United States to unilaterally and illegally impose a no-fly zone will lead to war with Russia.

In his editorial, Hof calls for total military backing for the Saudi-sponsored terrorists, including U.S. cruise missile strikes on the Syrian army and providing the terrorists with antiaircraft weapons to shoot down Russian planes.

Going Beyond Personal Justice

It is a matter of great urgency that the "heroes of the JASTA fight" take the next step in the battle for the future of the United States. In the aforementioned interview with Richard Black, the Senator points out that since 1991—that is, for 25 years (!)—the United States has dropped more than 294,000 bombs on the nation of Iraq, a neutral non-belligerent country which never attacked the United States and which had nothing what-

soever to do with the 9/11 attacks. And, as of today, we are continuing to drop those bombs. As of 2003, we have killed over 100,000 civilians in Iraq—men, women, children, the elderly and the disabled. By now the death toll is much higher. We have bombed their water plants, their power plants, their hospitals, and destroyed a large part of the infrastructure upon which human life depends. The death toll, as of 2016, is much higher.

All of this not only continued under the last seven and a half years of the Obama Presidency, it escalated and intensified. This is what our nation has come to. Americans must face this reality and not hide from it. This is what Obama's continued Presidency represents. These are the consequences of moral cowardice.

Also, as revealed in the British Inquiry into David Cameron and the overthrow of the Libyan government, the Obama administration, i.e., President Barack Obama personally, played the leading key role in the destruction of the Libyan nation and the pre-meditated murder of the Libyan head of state, Muammar Qaddafi. This alone is an impeachable offense.

Obama is now arming and supporting the very same Saudi-sponsored terrorist forces in Syria which conducted the 9/11 attacks killing American citizens.

But, even with that, we now stand on the precipice of something much worse, something truly terrible. We could be days or hours away from a U.S. military attack on Russian forces in Syria. We could be days or hours away from the imposition of a no-fly zone, which would unleash the U.S. military to shoot down Russian planes.

And remember, the Russians are there legally, at the request of the Syrian government. Everything the United States is doing in Syria is illegal, in violation of all international law and without Congressional approval.

Champions *are* needed. The JASTA veto exposed the moral rot and criminal actions of Barack Obama. The JASTA override proved what is possible if people stand for principle. The 25th Amendment provides the remedy, the way out, of this crisis.

Justice Victorious Over Obama's Veto: Which Side Is Germany On?

by Helga Zepp-LaRouche, chair of the German Civil Rights Movement Solidarity Party (BüSo)

Oct. 1—The devastating defeat which the U.S. Senate and House of Representatives dealt President Obama, with their overrides of his veto of the Justice Against Sponsors of Terrorism Act (JASTA), represents an historic opportunity to reappraise and rectify the entire catastrophic policy of the trans-Atlantic world since September 11, 2001. That must include the consequences of the wars in the Middle East and North Africa—based on lies—and the causes of the refugee crisis and terrorism.

The most important lesson to learn from these votes—which were the result of a 15-year, heroic struggle by the families of the victims of the attack on the World Trade Center—is this: Yes, we can indeed act to help achieve victory for justice! At the decisive moment, the passionate appeal of the victims' families to the Congressmen won out over the geopolitical manipulations and alliances of the Bush and Obama regimes.

As several of the family members stressed in interviews, for them this fight was not about what compensation they could get, but about justice for the people whom they have lost and about dismantling the cover-up of the true circumstances behind 9/11, a cover-up that provided the pretext for many wars in which millions of innocent people lost their lives and whole nations were virtually totally destroyed.

Given the dramatic escalation of the military situation in Syria and the confrontation between the United States and Russia, which threatens to escalate into a global war, this setback for Obama comes not a moment too soon. Russian President Vladimir Putin has obviously drawn his own conclusions from the Pentagon

LaRouche PAC organizers in New York City.

LPAC

and State Department's sabotage of the ceasefire process between Secretary of State John Kerry and Foreign Minister Sergei Lavrov. At exactly the point that Kerry and Lavrov had reached an agreement, there was a meeting in Washington of Obama, the Pentagon, the National Security Council, and the CIA, shortly after which the "unintentional" bombing of the Syrian army by U.S. air strikes occurred. In addition, the American side has not upheld its part of the Kerry-Lavrov agreement, namely, to separate the "moderate rebels" from the Islamic State and al-Nusra.

At the same time, the United States blamed Russia for the attack on an aid convoy, while Moscow blamed the terrorists. After the collapse of the ceasefire negotiations, the Syrian army reacted with the strongest attacks on the positions of the terrorist groups, which had by then deployed a strike force equivalent to two divisions of fighters in East Aleppo.

Ill-Concealed Threat Against Russia

Then on Sept. 28, State Department spokesman Rear Admiral (ret.) John Kirby predicted that extremists would attack Russian targets, perhaps even in Russian cities; that Russian soldiers would be brought home in body bags; and that more Russian airplanes would be shot down—a prediction the Russian side considered a blatant threat.

Admiral Kirby said, according to the official transcript of the State Department Daily Press Briefing of Sept. 28: "extremists and extremists groups will continue to exploit the vacuums that are there in Syria to expand their operations, which will include, no question, attacks against Russian interests, perhaps even Russian cities, and Russia will continue to send troops home in body bags, and they will continue to lose resources—even, perhaps, more aircraft."

Meanwhile U.S. Secretary of Defense Ashton Carter was visiting various military bases around the United States to make the case for Obama's trillion dollar program of modernization of nuclear weapons. At his first stop, at Minot Air Force Base in North Dakota, Carter announced, in front of a backdrop of a nuclear-capable B-52 bomber, that nuclear weapons have not been deployed since 1945, but that one should not take this for granted. He then proceeded to declare North Korea and Russia to be equal threats. The Russian Foreign Ministry reacted "with concern," noting that Carter's remarks meant that the U.S. would apparently be prepared to deploy nuclear weapons in an armed conflict which involved Russia, and that the United States is knowingly presenting a false picture of the content of the military doctrine Russia adopted in 2014.

More Air Strikes on Syrian Troops?

According to Reuters, the U.S. administration is now openly threatening air strikes against the Syrian army, while sections of the U.S. government have expressed fear that Russian soldiers could also be killed in such attacks. At the same time, American officials have pointed out that they could allow Turkey and Saudi Arabia to supply the Syrian rebels with anti-aircraft weapons. German author and journalist Jürgen Todenhöfer has, in the meantime, published interviews which he had conducted a short time before with an al-Nusra commander in Aleppo, in which this leader admitted that all the rebels' weapons came from the United States, and were then distributed by al-Nusra to different groups with constantly changing names.

September 11th was the evil deed which then "must give birth to perpetual evil," as it is said in Schiller's play, *The Piccolomini*—that is, the wars in Afghanistan, Iraq, Libya, and Syria, in which "regime change" was justified on the basis of misrepresentations. How long must we go on hearing the story of the "good rebels," who change their names and composition faster than weapons are delivered to them?

Instead of condemning the "barbaric" attack by the Syrian army on Aleppo based on this distortion, as Chancellor Merkel did after a telephone call with Obama—in order to play her intended role in a deceitful film—the Bundestag should urgently launch its own investigation into the implications of the "28 pages" and JASTA for understanding the causes setting in motion the refugee crisis and the terror attacks in Europe.

A New Paradigm to Prevent War

It as just as urgent to stop the confrontation with Russia—which could lead very quickly to a global thermonuclear war—as it is to get the immediate reorganization of the bankrupt financial system at long last on the agenda. The entire international financial press is full of panic articles, saying that the collapse of Deutsche Bank, whose stock fell to under 10 euros a share on Sept. 30, threatens to unleash a global meltdown, due to the entanglement of all the counterparties in Deutsche Bank's extensive 42 trillion euro derivatives bubble. Deutsche Bank is faced with its "Lehman Brothers" moment, they say. On Sept. 30 *Bloomberg News* quoted

Michael Ingram of BGC Partners in London: "We have a very connected financial system. A zombie financial system at some point translates into a zombie economy."

Obviously fearing the rage of the voters, Mrs. Merkel claimed a few days ago that the German government will not step in to rescue Deutsche Bank. No one believes that because everyone knows that the explosive power of Deutsche Bank is sufficient to plunge the global financial system into the abyss, and thus to also throw the world economy into absolute chaos. Immediately after Merkel's statement, hedge funds began to speculate on an upcoming government reorganization by selling short.

The only way to stop the threatened collapse of the world financial system is the immediate, temporary nationalization of Deutsche Bank, which must be taken over by an administrative commission. Its derivatives contracts must be unwound in an orderly fashion, that is, substantially written off. Then the bank must be provided with a new business plan in the tradition of Alfred Herrhausen, and thereby turned into a commercial bank for investing in industry. Because of the global scale of Deutsche Bank's operations, the implementation of the Glass-Steagall banking separation model in the Deutsche Bank case would provide a perfect starting point for the realization of a global Glass-Steagall system.

cc/Tobias Koch
Wolfgang Schäuble and Chancellor Angela Merkel in the German Bundestag, 2014.

Germany Must Stand Up for Itself

At the G-20 Summit in Hangzhou, China put on the agenda the perspective of both win-win cooperation in the world economy on the basis of innovation, and the necessity for a new financial architecture. The implementation of the New Silk Road, on which already more than 70 countries are collaborating, provides the concrete prospect for overcoming the world financial crisis and relaunching the world economy. Germany needs to join in.

Twenty-six years after German reunification, it is high time for Germany to stand up for its own sovereign interests. It should certainly be allowed, now that the European Union, of all entities, has rediscovered the virtues of national sovereignty and committed itself so clearly to the sovereignty of Saudi Arabia, as opposed to the rights of the family members of the victims of 9/11.

To make this possible, we need a new paradigm of thinking; we must hark back to the high point of our own culture, German Classical culture, in which music, poetry, and science blossomed. If we rise to the level of thinking on which geniuses such as Nicholas of Cusa, Kepler, Leibniz, Bach, Beethoven, Schiller, Einstein, and Krafft Ehricke thought, we will be able to awaken the sublime frame of mind and the creative optimism we need to find solutions on that higher level, the level on which these great souls thought.

And why shouldn't we be able to realize a renaissance of our humanistic tradition? In China they are celebrating the 2,567th birthday of Confucius by bringing to life his philosophy—which is very similar to European humanism in many respects—in all layers of society. In Germany, we have the good fortune of having an extraordinarily great number of poets, thinkers, and scientists who have contributed to universal history. We need only rediscover them. Our future can only lie in the ideal of a humanity which realizes the common goals of our species, goals expressed poetically and musically in Schiller's "Ode to Joy" and Beethoven's Ninth Symphony.